# Millau Viaduct

**Marty Gitlin**

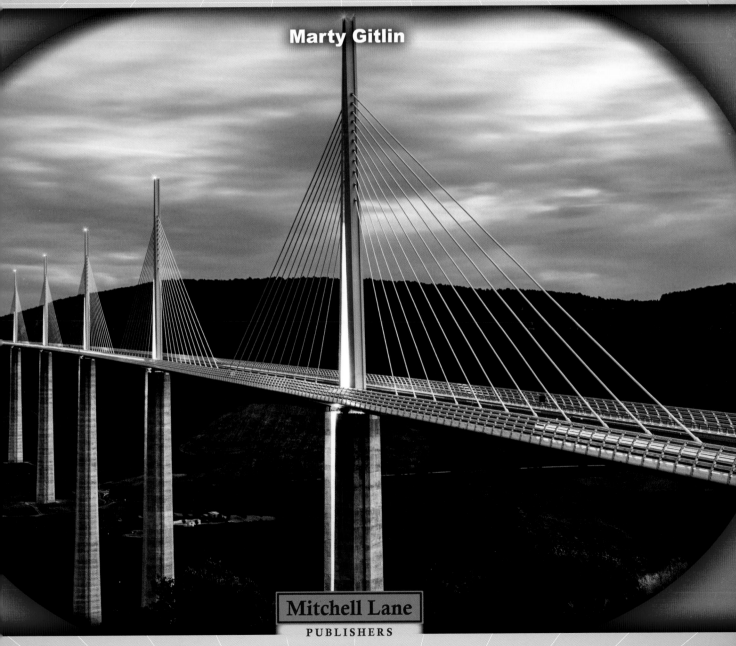

**Mitchell Lane**

PUBLISHERS

**2001 SW 31st Avenue
Hallandale, FL 33009
www.mitchelllane.com**

# Mitchell Lane
## PUBLISHERS

Printing        1        2        3        4        5        6        7        8

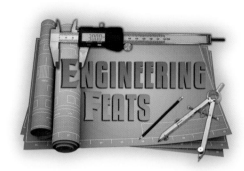

Designer: Sharon Beck
Editor: Jim Whiting

Library of Congress Cataloging-in-Publication Data
Names: Gitlin, Marty, author.
Title: The Millau Viaduct / by Marty Gitlin.
Description: Hallandale, FL : Mitchell Lane Publishers, 2018. | Series: Engineering feats | Includes bibliographical references and index. | Audience: Grades 4 to 6.
Identifiers: LCCN 2017046700 | ISBN 9781680201666 (library bound)
Subjects: LCSH: Viaduct de Millau (France)—Juvenile literature. | Viaducts—France—Millau— Juvenile literature. | Cable-stayed bridges—France—Millau—Juvenile literature.
Classification: LCC TG72.M54 G58 2018 | DDC 624.2/38094474—dc23
LC record available at https://lccn.loc.gov/2017046700

eBook ISBN: 9-781-68020-167-3

PHOTO CREDITS: Design elements—RED_SPY/Getty Images, Ifness/Getty Images, Madmaxer/Getty Images, chictype/Getty Images, Thissatan/Getty Images, Nongkran_ch/Getty Images. Back cover photos (left to right)—NASA/JPL, Imagine China/Newscom, Henryk Sadura/Getty Images, NASA, Rehman/cc by-sa 2.0, U.S. Navy/Mass Communication Specialist Seaman Casey Hopkins/Public domain. Cover, pp. 1, 32-33, 35 (inset)—Henryk Sadura/Getty Images; p. 4—JMarc_Stamati/Getty Images Plus; p. 6—NEBINGER-POOL/SIPA/ Newscom; p. 7—guichaoua/Alamy Stock Photo; p. 8—Tony Hisgett/Public domain; p. 9—Lyhne KRT/Newscom; p. 10—Roulex 45/GFDL/ cc-by-sa 3.0; p. 11—Frans Sellies/Getty Images; p. 13—AP Photo/Patrick Kovarik, Pool/Associated Press, (inset)—MOSSOT/cc-by-sa 3.0; pp. 14-15—Till Niermann/GFDL/cc-by-sa 3.0; p. 15—António Manuel da Fonseca/National Maritime Museum/Public domain; p. 17—Paste at English Wikipedia/Public domain; p. 19—Nepomuk at French Wikipedia/Public domain; pp. 20-21, 22-23—VIEW Pictures Ltd/Alamy Stock Photo; pp. 24-25—AP Photo/Claude Paris/Associated Press; p. 27—Anastasia traveller/Alamy Stock Photo; pp. 28-29—Gilles Paire/ Alamy Stock Photo; pp. 30-31—Hemis/Alamy Stock Photo; p. 35—mauritius images GmbH/Alamy Stock Photo; p. 36—Ross Jolliffe/Alamy Stock Photo; p. 37—Clem Rutter, Rochester Kent/GFDL/CC-BY 2.5; p. 38—spgd/Getty Images Plus; p. 39—Sion Touhig/Staff/Getty Images News.

# CONTENTS

Words in **bold** throughout can be found in the Glossary.

# 1

# One Beautiful Bridge

Imagine a jet plane zooming through the air over southern France. A young passenger is sound asleep. Suddenly her friend shakes from her slumber. "Quick! Look out there!" urges the friend. The girl glances out the window. She can hardly believe her eyes. A beautiful bridge below her is so tall that it seems to rise above the clouds.

"What is that?" she asks.

A man sitting behind her leans forward. "That's the Millau Viaduct," he says. "It is amazing."

It is indeed. The Millau Viaduct is the tallest bridge in the world, with one tower rising to a height of 1,125 feet (343 meters). It soars above the lush green Tarn River **Gorge**.

The incredible structure is made of steel and **concrete**. So it is very strong. But it does not appear thick and heavy. It looks thin and delicate.[1]

It is more than just a stunning work of art. It is as useful as it is gorgeous. The bridge helps link the French capital of Paris to the Mediterranean Sea and to Spain, where French citizens and foreign tourists frolic on sandy and sunny beaches.

The viaduct opened in 2004. No longer do drivers have to contend with cars and trucks jamming the roads. They can relax and gaze down at the wonderful scenery.[2]

The plan for the bridge was conceived in 1987. The idea was motivated by traffic jams on the narrow streets of the town of Millau.

The stately Millau Viaduct rises beautifully above the Tarn River Gorge in the Aveyron region of France.

Drivers got sick of being stuck. So did the town's 22,000 residents. All of them were forced to drive through one 20-mile stretch in and out of the valley. They were often stopped dead in traffic during the summer. It could take hours to drive those 20 miles.[3]

The decision to build the viaduct was not made until 1991. Its **construction** finally began in 2001. Three years later, on December 14, 2004, French president Jacques Chirac stood proudly at the building site. He was surrounded by workers who had built the bridge. They came from France, Spain, Italy, and Sweden. They met and defeated many challenges.[4] Chirac lifted a French flag as fighter jets roared overhead, leaving a trail of red, white, and blue smoke. He praised one and all for a job well done.

French president Jacques Chirac unveils a plaque during a ceremony that celebrated the opening of the Millau Viaduct on December 14, 2004.

# FAST FACT ✏

Why did the fighter jets helping celebrate the opening of the Millau Viaduct leave a trail of red, white, and blue smoke? Those are the colors of the French flag. It shares the same colors as the American flag. But it is quite different in design.

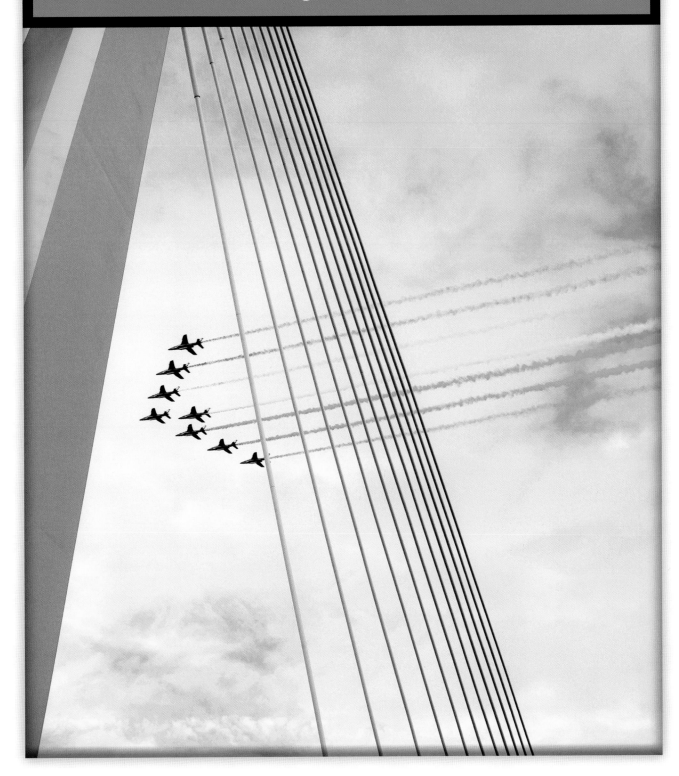

This photo of the Millau Viaduct provides a wonderful view of the French countryside that gives a backdrop to its beauty.

## Millau viaduct: World's tallest bridge

Designed by Briton Sir Norman Foster and built by the Eiffel Tower contractors, this elegant French bridge will form part of the A75 highway linking Paris to the Mediterranean.

Tarn River

Bridge

**Tallest point:** 343 m (1,125 ft.)

Bridge  Eiffel Tower

250 km
250 miles

**FRANCE**  GERMANY
Paris ★

Bay of Biscay

A71

SWITZ.

A75

**Bridge**  • Millau  ITALY

SPAIN  Med. Sea

© 2003 KRT
Source: Eiffage - Viaduc de Millau
Graphic: Jutta Scheibe, Morten Lyhne

**Length:** 2,460 m (1.53 mi.)

**Cost:** 320 mil. euros ($377 mil.)

**Construction time:** 39 months

**Road:** Two-lane dual highway; suspended almost 250 m (820 ft.) above Tarn River

**Completion:** Jan. 2005

**Pillars:** Seven; the tallest is 240 m (787 ft.)

**Steel used:** 36,000 metric tons (39,700 tons)

**Concrete used:** 206,000 metric tons (227,000 tons)

He spoke about what the viaduct meant to his country. He boasted that the bridge would go down in history as a great **engineering** feat.

The bridge rises from the ground like a part of nature. While man-made structures often ruin the surrounding scenery, many people believe the Millau Viaduct enhances the beauty of the French countryside.

**Diagram Comparing the Highest Pier (P2)
of the Millau Viaduct in France with the Eiffel Tower**

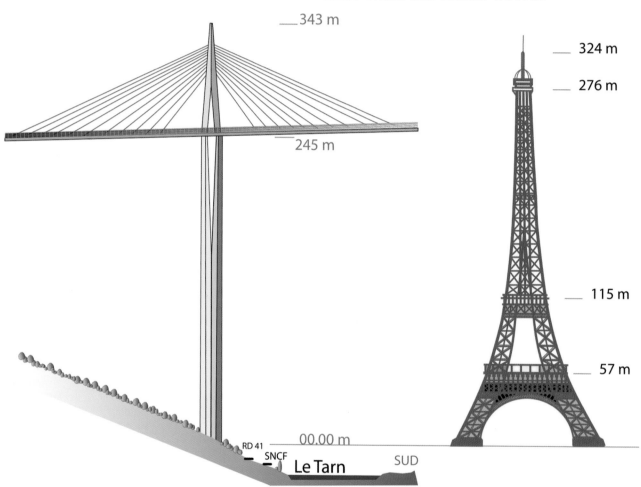

FAST FACT ✏

A company named Eiffage built the Millau Viaduct. Eiffage also built the famous Eiffel Tower in Paris, which was completed in 1887. The Millau Viaduct is often called the "Eiffel Tower of the South."

Among them is British architect Sir Norman Foster, who helped design it. He did so with the intention of blending it in with the scenery. "A work of man must fuse with nature," Foster said. "The pillars had to look almost organic, like they had grown from the earth."[5]

Nearly five million vehicles cross the Millau Viaduct every year. For many drivers, the crossing is similar to a short pleasure cruise. They take pictures of the amazing bridge and the beauty below. They snap photos of the canyons and valleys. They stare at the red soil and dark oak forests. It is no wonder that the speed limit is slightly lower on the bridge than on the roads leading up to it. That allows drivers to slow down and capture the moment. Drivers do not mind taking their time crossing it. The viaduct is not just eye candy. It also gets them faster and cheaper to their destinations. They spend nearly $30 less on tolls for light vehicles. And they travel 46 miles less from Paris to the southern French city of Perpignan.[6]

But any bridge can save time and money. The Millau Viaduct is unique in its size and splendor. It is not only the tallest bridge in the world. It is perhaps the most beautiful as well. And that is exactly what Foster had in mind. "Looking at it should provoke an emotion," he said. "Its purpose is to allow people to cross the valley without damaging the town of Millau. But it goes far beyond that."[7]

Millau Viaduct at night

The story of how the viaduct became a reality is amazing. So are the talents of its designers.

# 2

# The Stars of the Show

The Millau Viaduct is a tribute to the art of design. Its beauty confirms the creativity of two men: Michel Virlogeux and Norman Foster. They can be called designers. Or engineers. Or **architects**. They are among the best no matter how they are labeled. Virlogeux is French. Foster is British. But neither man limits his brilliance to his native country. Other nations throughout the world desire their great gifts. Their feats reflect their training. Both learned their craft at excellent schools. They gained a love for their jobs. Combined with their talents, that love has resulted in brilliant careers.

Virlogeux was born in the small French town of LaFleche in 1946. He graduated from two of the finest universities in France. He joined the French Highway Administration in 1974 and led its Bridge Division for 20 years. He worked on more than 100 bridges during that time. His greatest feat before the Millau Viaduct was the cable-stayed Normandy Bridge in France. In this type of construction, cables run directly from the towers to the roadway. That forms a fan-like pattern with the cables running nearly parallel to each other. That masterpiece over the River Seine between the coastal cities of Le Havre and Honfleur was completed in 1994. Its main span of 2,821 feet (857 meters) made it easily the longest cable-stayed bridge in the world. Virlogeux helped launch a new wave of bridge design. The building of longer spans is usually done in small stages. To attempt a span

French president Jacques Chirac (left) talks with British architect Sir Norman Foster during the 2004 inauguration of the viaduct. Foster and Frenchman Michel Virlogeux (inset) helped design the bridge.

that long was a leap into the unknown. It was unheard of anywhere in the world.

Virlogeux began a career as a project advisor in 1995. He worked on the Bastille Vertical Lift Bridge in France in 2013. He also helped design a bridge over the Panama Canal.[1]

## FAST FACT ✎

Among the bridges in other countries Michel Virlogeux helped build was the Vasco da Gama Bridge in Portugal. Da Gama was the first European explorer to reach India by sea. Though his voyage occurred more than 500 years ago, he is still remembered.

An aerial view of the Vasco da Gama Bridge in Lisbon, Portugal. It is the longest bridge in Europe. Construction began in February, 1995, and the bridge was opened to traffic in March, 1998.

Virlogeux has won many awards. He is recognized worldwide for his creativity.

The same holds true for Foster, who was born in Manchester, England, in 1935. He studied at its School of Architecture and City Planning. Foster performed brilliantly in the classroom. He earned a **fellowship** to Yale University in Connecticut, where he secured his master's degree.

Foster soon launched his own company, Foster Associates. It has remained in business for 50 years and is now known as Foster and Partners. It boasts about 1,500 employees. It works on projects around the world, such as planned cities, airports, banks, and private homes. Among Foster's most famous works is the renovation of the Reichstag in Berlin, Germany. That is the home of the German Parliament, the nation's legislative body. His company has won more than 400 awards.

Personal honors have also poured in. Foster earned Gold Medals for Architecture in England, France, and the United States. He won the Pritzker Architecture Prize

Vasco da Gama

in 1999. Many people consider this award as the Nobel Prize of architecture. He was even knighted by the queen of England! He is now addressed as Sir Norman Foster.[2]

The Millau Viaduct was the first such structure to be designed in part by an architect. The French government decided that it must be shaped by an architect as well as by an engineer. But the decision to hire Foster angered many French architects.

Foster had his own ideas. He wanted to build the bridge over the entire valley. The French architects believed it should only span the Tarn River. "I said . . . that I was definitely not the person that they should choose if they wanted to build a bridge across the river," Foster said. "I wanted to build a bridge to cross the whole valley. . . . Something that would be elegant and uniform and delicate and take account of the grandeur and sweep of the landscape."[3]

Foster has a firm grasp of every mission. He is aware that each one must please many people. He knows that what others want is important. He achieves that by listening, to gain a knowledge of their needs. Then he produces a plan in which he has confidence. "Creating a building involves the efforts and energy of thousands of people," Foster said. "So there is a massive task of communication. One has to be a totally committed optimist to not give up before even starting."[4]

Such was the case when he began work on the Millau Viaduct. Foster learned much about the ideas of Virlogeux. The French designer had already decided that it had to blend in with the beautiful countryside.

"I considered from the start that the site was very natural and very, very quiet," Virlogeux said. "I thought it was necessary to build a bridge that was very calm, very soft in character. It had to be very slender. And for that reason, the bridge had to be cable-stayed."[5] With that in mind, the two men went to work. What resulted is perhaps the greatest achievement in the history of bridge design.

## FAST FACT ✏

Norman Foster designed one of the most unusual office buildings in London, England. It is nicknamed the "Gherkin Building" for its strange form. A gherkin is a variety of cucumber used to make pickles. The structure is shaped like a gherkin cucumber.[6]

# 3

# A Job Well Done

The date was December 17, 2004. Photos of the Millau Viaduct had been splashed all over French newspapers. The media had praised it as a work of art.[1] Now the future had arrived. All the planning, all the designing, all the construction was done. The bridge was finally open for business. Cars and trucks rolled across it for the first time. Passengers eagerly took pictures as they passed.

Yet no one could forget the past. The viaduct's strength and beauty were the result of hard work by many people.

It had all started in 1991, when Virlogeux created his first designs. He later received plenty of help from Foster. But great architects cannot turn an idea into reality by themselves. Everyone who drove on the Millau Viaduct that first day had many other people to thank. They included:

- The **topographers** who studied the terrain to plan construction.
- The crane operators who moved tons of concrete and steel.
- The welders who pieced together metal parts to create the deck and the masts that support it.
- The site managers who ran the daily operations.
- The lift operators who ensured that workers were carried safely to the top of the **piers**.[2]

A pier is shown here during the early phases of construction. Each pier is supported by four deep shafts.

All of these workers—and many more—could now look with pride at what they had achieved. They viewed evidence everywhere of a job well done. They could see:

- A bridge with a total weight of 320,000 tons.
- A metallic deck that weighs nearly 36,000 tons.
- Eight spans that average more than 1,000 feet (about 305 meters) in length and 105 feet (31 meters) in width.
- Seven supporting masts that weigh more than 700 tons each.
- Twenty-two cables from each mast that support the deck. Each one has between 55 and 91 steel strands. All are triple protected against corrosion.[3]

A view from the south of the construction of the Millau Viaduct.

The workers had to overcome problems from the start. Construction began on October 10, 2001. But Mother Nature had other ideas. Terrible weather forced work to be suspended. It was two months before the first stone was laid down. The plan to build the bridge in three years appeared to be doomed.

The French government pushed back its deadline to January, 2005. But the workers quickly began making up for the lost time. The Millau Viaduct construction was completed in six stages.[4]

The first—and longest-lasting—stage was erecting the seven piers that support the structure. One of them rose 804 feet (245 meters), making it the highest pier in the world. This stage began in March, 2002 and was completed the following December.

The second stage began with assembling 36,000 tons of steel for the deck. The deck consists of 173 box beams more than 13 feet (4 meters) thick and laid end to end. These beams are criss-crossed with girders to support the weight of the road surface and the vehicles that pass along it. Two open sites were set up behind the piers. Almost all the welding and assembling was done there. That limited risk for 150 workers doing dangerous jobs at great heights. Workers began setting down the sections of the deck, starting at each end of the bridge, and slowly moving toward each other.

Stage three brought joy to the workers, when the two sections of the deck were joined on May 28, 2004. They met 886 feet (270 meters) above the Tarn River. The two ends of the bridge were at different heights, giving it a south-to-north slope, and the bridge design featured a slight curve. Yet the two sections aligned within less than a half-inch of each other!

Installing the seven masts marked the fourth stage. They were laid on the deck by trucks, then placed upright over the concrete piers. The operation took just three months.

## FAST FACT ✏

One feature of the viaduct is advanced sensors. They sense movement and motion in the bridge. Data collected from them help engineers locate trouble spots such as wear and tear. Those problems could shorten the life of bridge parts if not detected.[5]

The fifth stage was attaching the cable stays. Each mast of the bridge was equipped with 11 pairs of stays. They were laid face to face.

Surfacing the deck with asphalt ended the process. About 22 million pounds were poured onto the steel over a four-day period in September 2004 and then smoothed. Its thickness was just over two and a half inches (6.7 centimeters). Among the finishing touches were two weather stations. They judge conditions over the viaduct and the toll gate.

The job was finished ahead of schedule. Even with the delay caused by bad weather in 2001, the entire project required just 38 months. French officials had feared that the total cost would be over budget. But it came in at under $523 million. That was less than the original estimate. And soon the viaduct was open for traffic. It was a sight to behold.

An east view of the construction of the Millau Viaduct.

This photo shows the Millau Viaduct roadway upon its completion in May, 2004. It opened to traffic seven months later.

# 4

# Worth the Wait

A common saying is that beauty is in the eyes of the beholder. And few who have seen the Millau Viaduct deny its beauty. The stunning view is not all that makes it different. It is also unusually designed. Most bridges are suspension bridges. Their main cables hang between pillars near each end. A series of smaller vertical cables are connected to the main cable at one end and the deck at the other. In turn, the two pillars are connected to the ground on each end.

The Millau Viaduct is a cable-stayed bridge. Cable-stayed bridges have one or more masts with cables supporting the deck. They can have a fan or harp design. The cables in a fan bridge all connect to the top of the mast. Harp bridge cables are attached to various points on the mast and run nearly **parallel** to each other to the deck. The Millau Viaduct has this design.

French planners had originally considered four bridge types. They also considered digging a tunnel beneath the Tarn Gorge. Another option was constructing four separate spans. The planners decided in 1989 to build one bridge just east of Millau. They chose a cable-stayed design in 1996.

It was not completed for another eight years. But it was worth the wait. Its design received rave reviews. Experts in the field were very impressed. Among them was Jonathan Glancey, who writes about architecture for a British newspaper. He praised the viaduct as

The cables and outer guard rails of the cable-stayed Millau Viaduct are shown here. The cable-stayed structure shown in the inset is the Russky Bridge in Vladivostok, Russia. That bridge has the second-highest masts behind the Millau Viaduct and the longest cable stays.

an "epic work of art." He compared its amazing design to cathedrals that dated back hundreds of years. He added that its greatness extends far beyond its purpose.[1]

That purpose is to help people get places faster. That means it must be durable and capable of withstanding several weather conditions. It is exposed to the hot sun during the summer and must withstand winter winds of 100 miles (160 kilometers) an hour. The roadway surface was designed to expand or contract by as much as 10 feet (3 meters). Clear screens standing 3 meters (nearly 10 feet) tall along its sides shield drivers from high winds. They enhance the beauty of the bridge as well.

Eiffage agreed to finance their work. But they received 75 years of toll collections in return. The French government can take over the bridge

tolls in 2044. It will do that if they are turning a large profit. The tolls are indeed bringing in plenty of money. It costs car drivers $9.30 every time they cross the bridge. That toll rises to nearly $12 during the peak summer vacation period. Truck drivers pay more than $41 for each crossing.[2] However, pedestrians and bicyclists cannot use the viaduct.

## FAST FACT

Drivers must pay a lot of money to drive over the Millau Viaduct. But they rarely wait long to pay their tolls. Eight toll booths in each direction make certain that drivers quickly get onto the viaduct.

Not all drivers use the Millau Viaduct. Some still opt for the N9 highway through town. They believe they are saving on tolls. Others realize that some of their money will be spent anyway on gas. Using the viaduct cuts down greatly on time and mileage. But they do not spend money just to get from one side to the other. They pay to see one of the most famous bridges in the world. They pay to see a work of art. They pay to view the beautiful scenery.

The viaduct has become a major Millau **landmark**. It is the town's prime attraction. It has also placed a spotlight on the French region of Aveyron. Before the bridge was built, most people knew little about the peaceful and beautiful area. Now people flock there to view and photograph the viaduct.[3]

And Millau has reaped the benefits. Tourists shop along its narrow, winding streets. Stores stock many items specifically related to the Millau

Viaduct, such as photos, books, postcards, calendars, puzzles, magnets, cups, and T-shirts with its image. A local newspaper praising the viaduct has even been published.

Millau had never received such attention. It did not attract tourists despite its beauty and the stunning countryside. Now the viaduct is to Millau as the Eiffel Tower is to Paris. People come from all over the world to gaze at it.

Sometimes visitors get lucky. That happens when the morning fog from the Tarn Valley rises and surrounds the bridge deck. Drivers have the sensation of moving through the sky.[3]

More than a decade has passed since the Millau Viaduct opened. And it remains a French treasure. People even came out to celebrate its birthday.

**A view of the town of Millau and the viaduct rising behind it.**

# 5

# A Bridge Party

It was December 14, 2014. Exactly 10 years had passed since French president Jacques Chirac had welcomed the Millau Viaduct into the world. People were ready to celebrate. Fireworks lit up the night sky over Millau in a celebration organized by town officials.

They had ample reason to rejoice. The incredible bridge had already welcomed nearly 50 million vehicles. One and all had learned of its benefits. The Millau Viaduct had always saved them at least 30 minutes of driving time. But it had saved them up to four hours on some summer weekends. They no longer had to drive bumper-to-bumper through the narrow and winding roads of Millau.

Truckers were especially thankful. Their daily or weekly routes to major cities in France, Spain, and the Netherlands were shortened. They had saved 45 minutes traveling to and from Paris, Barcelona, or Amsterdam. That meant getting their work done faster. It meant more money in their pockets. It meant more time spent with their families. The bridge did not just save them time. It saved them money. Sitting in traffic along the streets of Millau burned fuel. Trucks quickly gulped down gas. Rising gas prices made those journeys even more expensive. Whizzing through the Millau Viaduct allowed them to keep gas money in their pockets.

The first trip on a bridge so high in the sky might be scary. But the bridge was installed with safety features. Its strong barriers withstand the impact of trucks. Screens limit the effect of heavy winds on

Bustling traffic that includes cars in the main photo and a truck in the inset can be seen rolling across the Millau Viaduct.

vehicles. Emergency lanes sit 10 feet wide. The bridge is also equipped with emergency phones every 511 meters (about 550 yards).

A control center constantly monitors the viaduct. Video cameras link to a system that detects unusual traffic patterns. Weather stations eye severe conditions that hinder driving. Helpful information is relayed to drivers through an electronic message board.[1]

All the extras give drivers a sense of safety. It allows them to relax and enjoy the scenery. But the Millau Viaduct attracts more than just drivers. Its income extends beyond tolls. One million visitors stop at its tourist site every year. Its two information centers bring in about a half-million more. People spend lots of money to see the landmark. They can walk or drive under it. They can take a bus or boat trip to see it from ground level. They can even fly over it in a helicopter.

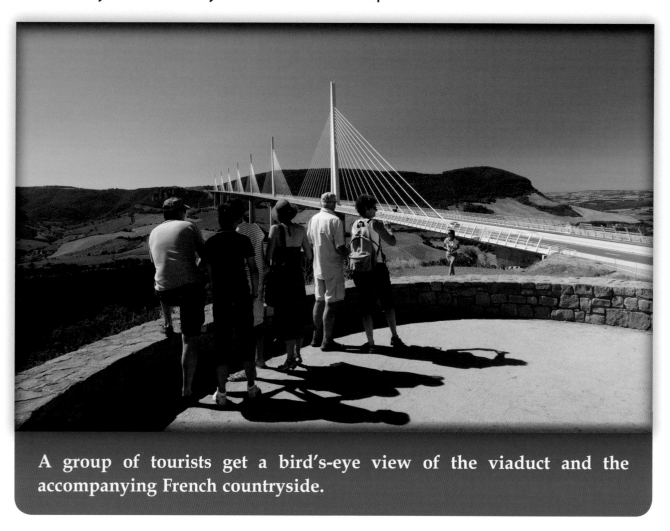

A group of tourists get a bird's-eye view of the viaduct and the accompanying French countryside.

Many people stop at the rest area. It provides a wonderful view of the viaduct. A souvenir shop allows them to buy items related to the famous bridge. They can even dine on fancy food during the summer.

The area around the Millau Viaduct has been transformed into quite the tourist attraction. Among the attractions shown here are a restaurant tent and visitors center.

The Viaduct Exhibition is a museum for curious visitors. Its displays and images teach people all about the bridge. A guided tour tells the story of the viaduct in six different languages. It allows people to explore the site. It also provides a view beneath the deck and the stunning surrounding scenery.

# FAST FACT ✎

The central mast on the Millau Viaduct that rises 1,125 feet (343 meters) into the air is taller than some of the most famous tall buildings in the world. It is taller than the Eiffel Tower in Paris and the Big Ben clock tower in London. It is almost as tall as the Empire State Building in New York City.

The entire country has embraced the Millau Viaduct. It is has become so iconic that it generated a 2016 television special called *Millau, The Impossible Viaduct*. Nearly 700,000 viewers watched it on BBC World-wide France. It marked the largest audience ever for a show on that network. The **documentary** traced how the bridge became a reality. It showed how Virlogeux and Foster worked together to create an amazing design. It also explained how early fears of failure were turned into an incredible success. Many people responsible for making it happen spoke about the process.[2]

People might think a bridge is just a bridge. They are often right. Its purpose is simply to help drivers get from one place to another.

But the Millau Viaduct is far more than just a bridge. It is a work of art. It can make people feel like they are driving in the sky. It allows them to feast their eyes on the beautiful countryside below. It is no wonder France is so proud of its great landmark.

**FAST FACT**

One of the biggest events in Millau before the viaduct was built centered on its McDonald's. In 1999, area farmer/activist José Bové and his followers damaged the fast food restaurant as it was being constructed. They were protesting the processed food McDonald's sells and many other issues. Bové spent time in jail for his actions. But he became a hero to many French people who agreed with his views.[3] He even ran for president in 2007.

# WHAT YOU SHOULD KNOW

★ It is the tallest bridge in the world at 1,125 feet (343 meters).

★ A viaduct is a bridge consisting of several short spans.

★ The Millau Viaduct hovers over the Tarn River Gorge.

★ The French town of Millau had been plagued with traffic problems until they were relieved by the construction of the viaduct.

★ The decision to build the bridge was made in October 1991, after four years of consideration.

★ The Millau Viaduct was designed by French engineer Michel Virlogeux and British architect Sir Norman Foster.

★ The viaduct boasts a cable-stayed style instead of the more common suspension style. A cable-stayed bridge features multiple cables from each mast supporting a section of the bridge around the mast.

★ Construction of the Millau Viaduct did not begin until 2001.

★ Bad weather suspended construction for two months early in the process.

★ Despite weather issues, the bridge was completed in less time than first expected.

★ A ceremony featuring French president Jacques Chirac officially opened the bridge on December 14, 2014, and it opened for traffic three days later.

★ The viaduct has seven masts that are 285 feet (87 meters) high and weigh 700 tons each.

★ The tallest pier on the bridge stands nearly 804 feet (245 meters). It broke the record for the tallest pier in the world by about 170 feet (52 meters).

★ The Millau Viaduct cost about $523 million to build. That was less than what was budgeted.

★ The second-tallest bridge in the world is the Russky Bridge in Russia. It is 72 feet shorter than the Millau Viaduct.

★ The viaduct has a deck height of 886 feet (270 meters). That ranks 15th in the world, but it is the highest in Europe.

★ The roadway on the bridge is 8,071 feet (2,460 meters) in length. It takes about a minute and a half to drive across.

★ The speed limit on the Millau Viaduct had to be slightly reduced because too many drivers were slowing down to take pictures of the bridge and the scenery below.

★ The total weight of the bridge is about 640 million pounds (320,000 tons).

★ More than 50 million vehicles have passed over the Millau Viaduct since it opened in 2004.

★ Unlike many other bridges, pedestrians are not allowed on the Millau Viaduct.

★ The viaduct has several unique features, including motion sensors and slopes that give drivers a better view of what is ahead of them.

★ Norman Foster became involved in the project when the French government decided to use an architect as well as an engineer on the design.

# QUICK STATS

★ About 4.8 million vehicles drive over the Millau Viaduct every year

★ The shortest pier is 253 feet (77 meters)

★ The road thickness is 13 feet, 9 inches (4.2 meters)

★ The total weight of the bridge is 320,000 tons

**1987**   The first plans of a bridge are discussed.

**1991**   The decision to build a crossing over the River Tarn is made.

**1995**   Competition begins for bridge designers.

**1996**   A cable-stayed design is decided upon.

**2000**   A competition is launched to find the construction company.

**2001**   Eiffage is declared the winner of the competition and earns the construction contract. Construction on the viaduct begins.

**2002**   The assembly of the roadway begins. The first piers are completed. The first sections of roadway are laid.

**2003**   The last piers are completed.

**2004**   The two sections of roadway are joined. The Millau Viaduct opens to traffic ahead of schedule after its official inauguration.

**2007**   A footrace across the bridge known as the Course Eiffage du Viaduc de Millau is held for the first time and closes the bridge for four hours.

**2015**   The container ship *Millau Bridge* begins service with the K Line shipping company.

**2017**   Millau Viaduct architect Norman Foster designs a new line of bicycle clothing.

**Chapter 1: One Beautiful Bridge**

1. Jack Lyne, "World's tallest suspension bride opens in south France — on schedule, within budget." Snapshot. January 3, 2005. http://siteselection.com/ssinsider/snapshot/sf050103.htm

2. "Millau Viaduct." Highest Bridges. http://www.highestbridges.com/wiki/index.php?title=Millau_Viaduct

3. John Lichfield, "The mother of all bridges." *The Independent*. October 24, 2004. http://www.independent.co.uk/news/world/europe/the-mother-of-all-bridges-535416.html

4. "Millau Viaduct." Highest Bridges. http://www.highestbridges.com/wiki/index.php?title=Millau_Viaduct

5. "France shows off tallest bridge." BBC News. December 14, 2004. http://news.bbc.co.uk/1/hi/world/europe/4091813.stm

6. Viaduc de Millau. http://www.leviaducdemillau.com/en/getting-around/toll-charges

7. Lyne, "World's tallest suspension bride opens in south France — on schedule, within budget."

**Chapter 2: The Stars of the Show**

1. "Michel Virlogeux." Bridges of Dublin. http://www.bridgesofdublin.ie/bridge-building/bridge-designers/michel-virlogeux

2. "Biography." The Pritzker Architecture Prize. http://www.pritzkerprize.com/1999/bio

3. John Lichfield, "The mother of all bridges." *The Independent*. October 24, 2004. http://www.independent.co.uk/news/world/europe/the-mother-of-all-bridges-535416.html

4. "Full biography." The Pritzker Architecture Prize. http://www.pritzkerprize.com/sites/default/files/file_fields/field_files_inline/1999_bio_0.pdf

5. "High-wire artist." *The Engineer*. September 2008. https://www.theengineer.co.uk/issues/1-september-2008/high-wire-artist/

6. "30 St. Mary Axe: The Gherkin." Design Book Magazine. http://www.designbookmag.com/thegerkin.htm

## Chapter 3: A Job Well Done

1. "France opens world's tallest bridge." NBC News. Associated Press. http://www.nbcnews.com/id/6711265/ns/world_news/t/france-opens-worlds-tallest-bridge/#.Wa2OY8h942w

2. "The women and men of the viaduct." Viaduc de Millau. http://www.leviaducdemillau.com/en/understand/women-and-men-viaduct

3. "Millau Viaduct." Highest Bridges. http://www.highestbridges.com/wiki/index.php?title=Millau_Viaduct

4. "Construction in six stages." Viaduc de Millau. http://www.leviaducdemillau.com/en/understand/construction-six-stages

5. "Millau Viaduct." Highest Bridges.

## Chapter 4: Worth the Wait

1. Jack Lyne, "World's tallest suspension bride opens in south France — on schedule, within budget." Snapshot. January 3, 2005. http://siteselection.com/ssinsider/snapshot/sf050103.htm

2. "Toll charges." Viaduc de Millau. http://www.leviaducdemillau.com/en/getting-around/toll-charges

3. "The view from here: The stunning Millau Viaduct: Engineers take second billing again." Structural Engineering News. February 19, 2014. https://csengineermag.com/article/the-view-from-here-the-stunning-millau-viaduct-engineers-take-second-billing-again/

## Chapter 5: A Bridge Party

1. "The beautiful Millau Viaduct in France opens for traffic." DC Views. http://www.dcviews.com/press/Millau-Viaduct.htm

2. "Millau, the viaduct of the impossible." Atlantis Television. http://www.atlantistv.fr/emissions/15859/

3. "Millau Viaduct – highest cable-stayed bridge." Travel France online. https://travelfranceonline.com/millau-viaduct-highest-cable-stayed-bridge/

4. Wayne Northcutt, "Jose Bove vs. McDonald's: The making of a national hero in the French anti-globalization movement." *Journal of the Western Society for French History*. Volume 31 2003. https://quod.lib.umich.edu/w/wsfh/0642292.0031.020?rgn=main;view=fulltext

Charles River Editors. *The Golden Gate Bridge: The History of San Francisco's Most Famous Bridge*. North Charleston, SC: CreateSpace Independent Publishing Platform, 2015.

Cruickshank, Dan. *Dan Cruickshank's Bridges: Heroic Designs that Changed the World*. New York: Collins, 2010.

Foster, Norman. *Millau Viaduct*. Munich, Germany: Prestel Publishing, 2012.

Hurley, Michael. *The World's Most Amazing Bridges*. Mankato, MN: Raintree, 2011.

Latham, Donna. *Bridges and Tunnels: Investigate Feats of Engineering with 25 Projects*. White River Junction, VT, Nomad Press, 2012.

## WORKS CONSULTED

"30 St. Mary Axe: The Gherkin." Design Book Magazine. http://www.designbookmag.com/thegerkin.htm

"Construction in six stages." Viaduc de Millau. http://www.leviaducdemillau. com/en/understand/construction-six-stages

"France opens world's tallest bridge." NBC News. http://www.nbcnews.com/ id/6711265/ns/world_news/t/france-opens-worlds-tallest-bridge/#. Wa2OY8h942w

"France shows off tallest bridge." BBC News. December 14, 2004. http://news. bbc.co.uk/1/hi/world/europe/4091813.stm

"High-wire artist." *The Engineer*. September 2008. https://www.theengineer. co.uk/issues/1-september-2008/high-wire-artist/

Lichfield, John. "The mother of all bridges." *The Independent*. October 24, 2004. http://www.independent.co.uk/news/world/europe/the-mother-of-all-bridges-535416.html

Lyne, Jack. "World's tallest suspension bride opens in south France – on schedule, within budget." Snapshot. January 3, 2005. http://siteselection. com/ssinsider/snapshot/sf050103.htm

"Michel Virlogeux." Bridges of Dublin. http://www.bridgesofdublin.ie/bridge-building/bridge-designers/michel-virlogeux

"Millau, the viaduct of the impossible." Atlantis Television. http://www. atlantistv.fr/emissions/15859/

"Millau Viaduct." Highest Bridges. http://www.highestbridges.com/wiki/index. php?title=Millau_Viaduct

"Millau Viaduct – highest cable-stayed bridge." Travel France online. https:// travelfranceonline.com/millau-viaduct-highest-cable-stayed-bridge/

"Millau Viaduct: 10 Facts on the Tallest Bridge in the World. Learnodo-newtonic.com. https://learnodo-newtonic.com/millau-viaduct-facts

"Norman Foster: Biography." The Pritzker Architecture Prize. http://www. pritzkerprize.com/1999/bio

Northcutt, Wayne. "Jose Bove vs. McDonald's: The making of a national hero in the French anti-globalization movement." *Journal of the Western Society for French History*. Volume 31 2003. https://quod.lib.umich.edu/w/ wsfh/0642292.0031.020?rgn=main;view=fulltext

"The beautiful Millau Viaduct in France opens for traffic." DC Views. http:// www.dcviews.com/press/Millau-Viaduct.htm

"The view from here: The stunning Millau Viaduct: Engineers take second billing again." Structural Engineering News. February 19, 2014. https:// csengineermag.com/article/ the-view-from-here-the-stunning-millau-viaduct-engineers-take-second-billing-again/

"The women and men of the viaduct." Viaduc de Millau. http://www. leviaducdemillau.com/en/understand/women-and-men-viaduct

"Toll charges." Viaduc de Millau. http://www.leviaducdemillau.com/en/getting-around/toll-charges

# ON THE INTERNET

Easy Science for Kids: Facts About Bridges for Kids
    http://easyscienceforkids.com/all-about-bridges/

Millau Viaduct: 10 Facts on the tallest bridge in the world.
    Learnodo-Newtonic.com. https://learnodo-newtonic.com/millau-viaduct-facts

Kidskonnect: Bridge Facts.
    https://kidskonnect.com/science/bridges/

**architect** (AHR-ki-tekt)—person who designs buildings

**concrete** (kahn-KREET)—hard, strong material made by mixing cement, sand, and broken rocks with water

**construction** (kuhn-STRUHK-shuhn)—act or process of building something

**corrosion** (kuh-ROH-zhuhn)—process of slowly breaking apart or rusting

**documentary** (dok-yoo-MEN-tuh-ree)—movie or TV show that tells a story about real people and events

**engineer** (en-juh-NEER)—person with scientific training who designs and builds structures such as bridges

**fellowship** (FEL-oh-ship)—amount of money given to a university student to do research

**gorge** (GOHRG)—deep, narrow area between hills or mountains

**landmark** (LAND-mahrk)—a feature, either natural or manmade, that is easy to see and recognize

**parallel** (PAR-uh-lel)—lines or objects that are the same distance apart along their whole length and do not touch at any point

**piers** (PEERZ)—upright supports for a bridge

**tolls** (TOHLZ)—money paid to cross a bridge or highway

**topographer** (toe-PAHG-ruh-fer)—person who makes maps that show the height or shape of a piece of land

Marty Gitlin is an educational book author based in Cleveland, Ohio. He has published more than 120 books since 2006. He won numerous awards in 11 years as a newspaper journalist. One was first place for general excellence from the Associated Press. That organization also selected him as one of the top four feature writers in Ohio.